DISCARDED

TOM HANKS

by
Jill C. Wheeler

A&D BIOGRAPHIES
Star Tracks

REEVES ROGERS LIBRARY

Visit us at
www.abdopub.com

Published by ABDO Publishing Company, 4940 Viking Drive, Edina, MN 55435. Copyright ©2001 by Abdo Consulting Group, Inc. International copyrights reserved in all countries. No part of this book may be reproduced in any form without written permission from the publisher.

Printed in the United States.

Graphic Design: John Hamilton
Cover Design: MacLean Tuminelly
Cover photo: Shooting Stars
Interior photos:
  20th Century Fox, p. 54
  Amblin Entertainment and Universal Pictures, p. 34
  Amblin Entertainment and Warner Brothers, p. 45
  AP/Wide World, p. 1, 25, 32, 39, 41, 50, 53, 55, 59
  Corbis, p. 6, 9, 16, 19, 22, 27, 29, 31, 35, 36, 44, 47, 49, 57, 60-61, 63
  DreamWorks SKG and 20th Century Fox, p. 58
  Gracie Films and 20th Century Fox, p. 40
  Imagine Entertainment and Universal Pictures, p. 54
  Miller Milkis-Boyett Productions and Paramount Television, p. 24
  Shooting Stars, p. 5, 11, 14-15, 21, 42-43
  Time Pix, p. 13, 56
  Touchstone Pictures and Walt Disney Productions, p. 28

Library of Congress Cataloging-in-Publication Data
Wheeler, Jill C., 1964-
    Tom Hanks / Jill C. Wheeler.
        p. cm. — (Star tracks)
    Includes index.
    ISBN 1-57765-554-0
      1. Hanks, Tom—Juvenile literature. 2. Actors—United States—Biography—Juvenile literature. [1. Hanks, Tom. 2. Actors and actresses.] I. Title. II. Series

PN2287.H18 W48 2001
791.43'028'092—dc21
[B]   00-069991

CONTENTS

Hollywood's Leading Man 4

On the Road Again 8

Smitten by Shakespeare 12

Bosom Buddies 20

Making a *Splash* 26

Hits and Misses 30

A Fine Romance 37

Comeback 40

And the Oscar Goes to… 48

In the Director's Chair 52

Maximum Star Power 56

Where on the Web? 62

Glossary 63

Index 64

HOLLYWOOD'S LEADING MAN

IN THE DAYS BEFORE MOST PEOPLE HAD television, they had the movies. That was Hollywood's golden era. Stars like Jimmy Stewart and Cary Grant lit up the silver screen each week at the local cinema. Their light-hearted comedies gave everyone a couple of hours to forget their troubles.

These actors were very popular. Yet they also were people the average American could admire. Their down-to-earth manner and less-than-perfect looks made them seem even more likable. They were the good guys who didn't always finish last.

Television ended Hollywood's golden years. Movies became more extreme in order to compete with TV shows. Movie stars became even more glamorous. It seemed as though the magic of old Hollywood had vanished.

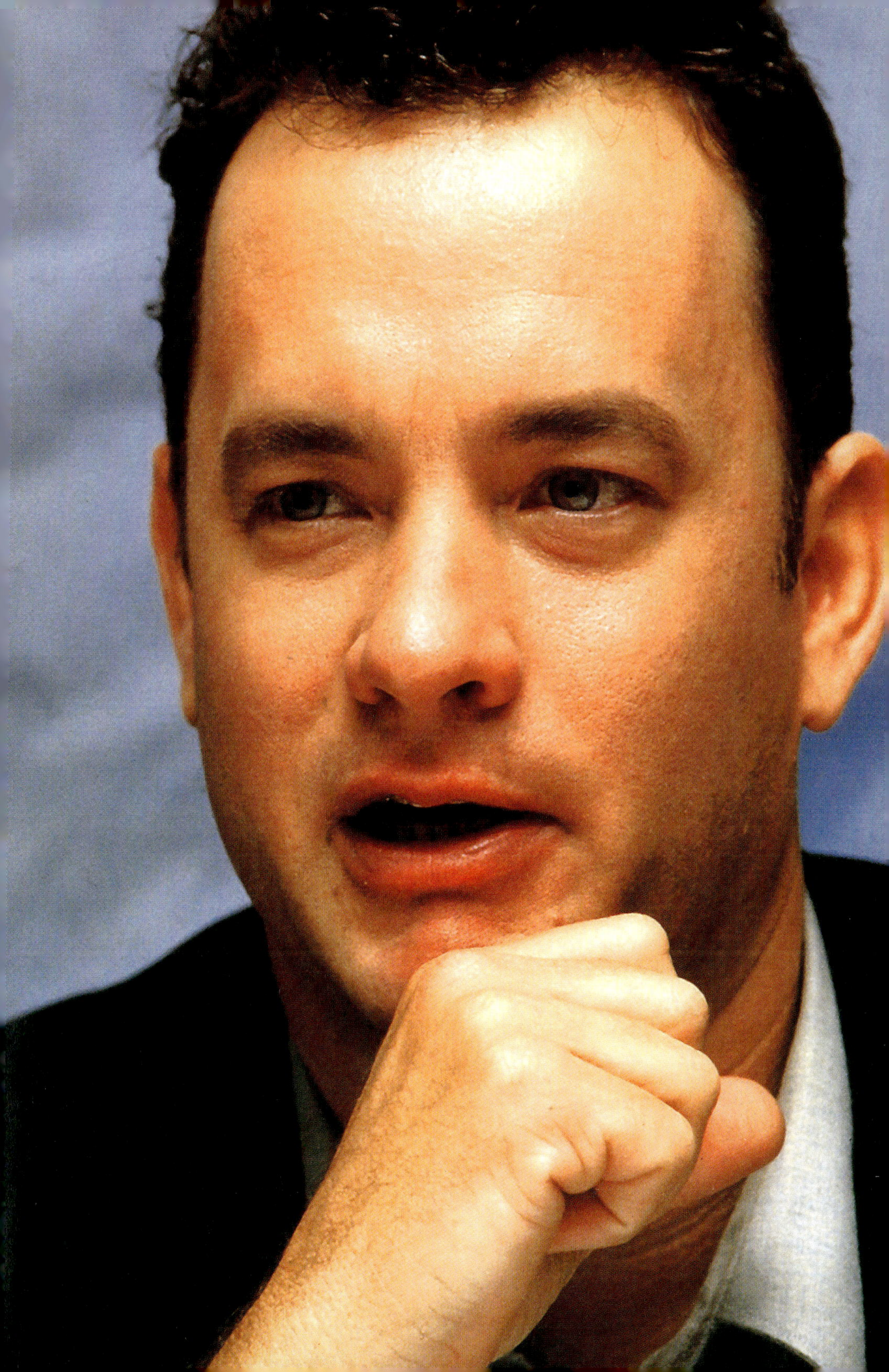

Tom Hanks, nominated for a Best Actor award for Saving Private Ryan, *and his wife Rita Wilson arrive March 21, 1999, at the 71st Annual Academy Awards in Los Angeles.*

Then in the 1980s, a fresh new actor came along. Though not handsome by most standards, he had a spark that drew people. He could deliver a line in between charming and arrogant—and get away with it. He played the nice guy next door who still got the girl.

"Despite his success, Tom Hanks has stayed much like the boy next door."

He was Tom Hanks. Self-described as "goofy-looking," Tom has won fans all over the world. His performances have ranged from hilarious to heart wrenching and everything in between. Despite his success, he's stayed much like the boy next door.

"It's rare that you find such a talented person who doesn't have an attitude," says Penny Marshall, who directed Tom in *A League of Their Own*. Adds Ron Howard, who directed Tom in *Splash*, "I think of him as a terrific leading man, like Jack Lemmon or Jimmy Stewart—funny guys who make you care."

Audiences have cared about Tom since he hit the small screen in 1980. Today, he's still making movies and new fans. Here's a glimpse at the story of Hollywood's leading man.

ON THE ROAD AGAIN

TOM HANKS WAS BORN ON JUNE 9, 1956, in Concord, California, to Amos and Janet Hanks. He was the third of four children. His father was a chef, and his mother was a hospital worker. His parents divorced when Tom was five years old. He and his older siblings went to live with his father.

Amos rarely stayed in one place very long. As a chef, it was easy for him to find different work. Everywhere he went, young Tom came along. "My dad was in the restaurant business, so, at a moment's notice, we'd be gone, packed up, and out of there," Tom recalls. The family moved many times around the San Francisco Bay area while Tom was growing up.

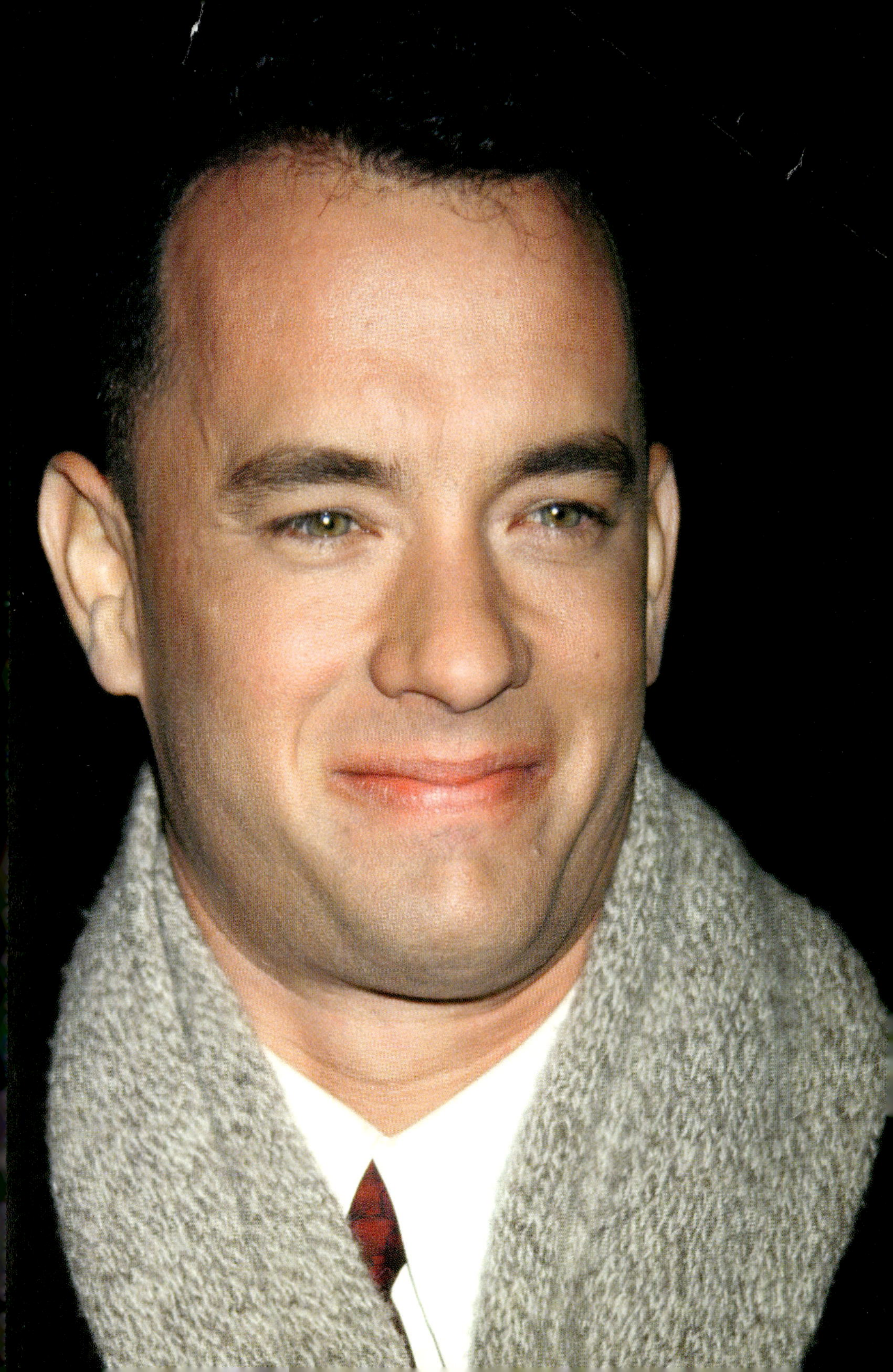

Such a nomadic lifestyle might have been hard on a young child. Yet Tom adapted and flourished. "It was great," he said. "I never got into trouble. I never had problems making friends."

Tom said the constant changes also taught him to be flexible. "I never thought twice about picking up, changing schools and cities," he said. "I came to like it a lot because there were always new things to discover." All in all, he attended at least five different elementary schools during his early years.

While Tom made friends quickly, he never had the time to create lasting friendships. As a result, he became somewhat shy. He relied on his keen sense of humor and sharp one-line wisecracks to warm up to people. "Being funny was a way to even the playing field," he recalls. He was elected "class cut-up" in his high school in Oakland.

It was at Skyline that Tom discovered the world of theater. Initially he wanted to learn about the technical side of theater, such as building sets and running the lights. He ended up taking a role in the high school production of *South Pacific*. After graduation, he enrolled in Chabot Junior College in Hayward, California.

"Being funny was a way to even the playing field."

SMITTEN BY SHAKESPEARE

AT CHABOT, TOM SIGNED UP FOR A CLASS called Drama in Performance. "I was tired of zoology and sociology," he explained. He and the other students thought it was an acting class. In reality, the class was about plays—reading them and seeing them performed. Within weeks, he knew he'd found something special.

"I thought going to see a play was a great way to spend an evening." he said. "I was just swept away, really shaken… impressed by how actors could get up on the stage and communicate from a blueprint a guy had made 40 years before. Here it was, coming to life—you could almost reach out and touch it."

"I thought going to see a play was a great way to spend an evening."

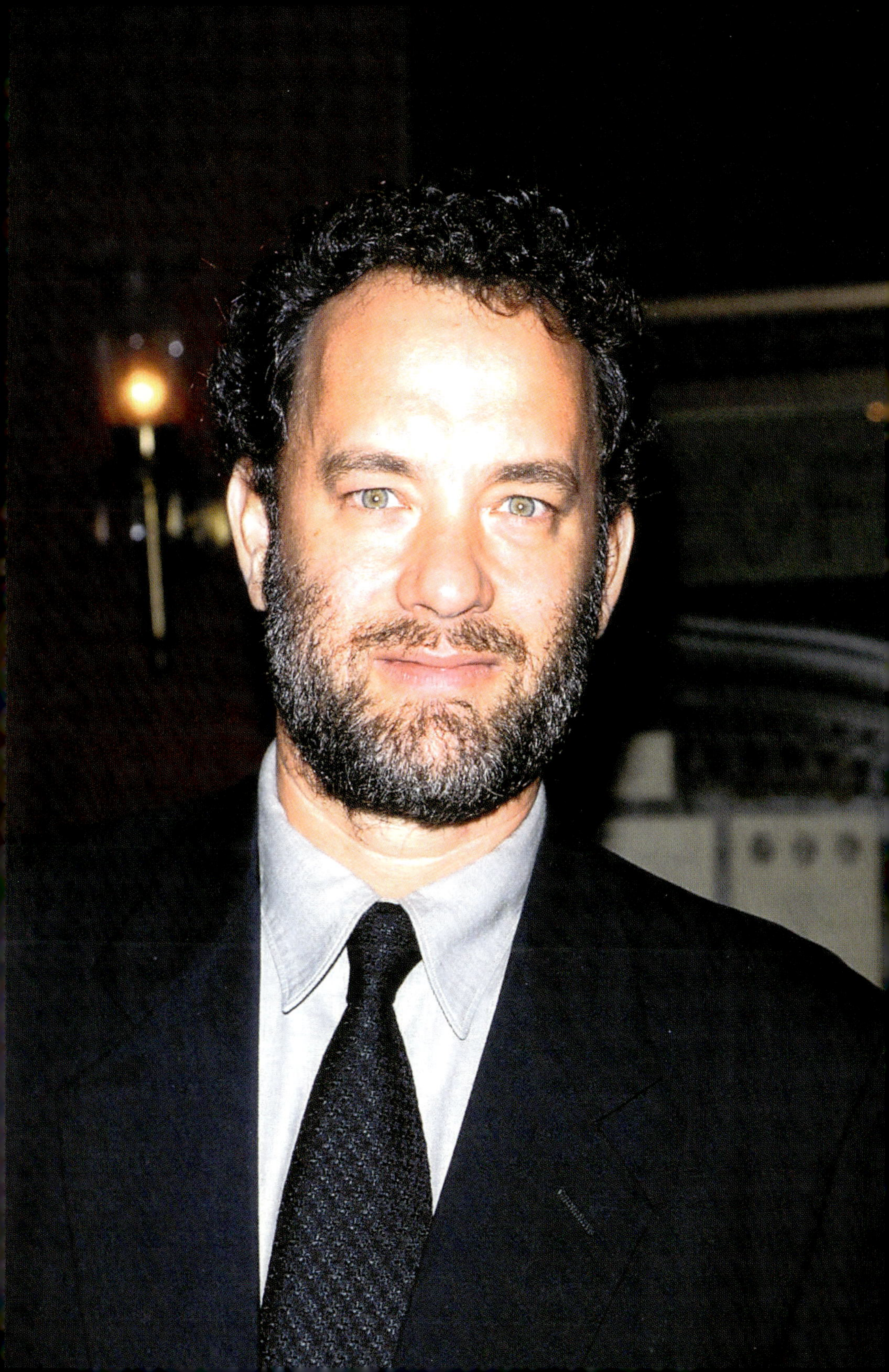

One night Tom saw the play *The Iceman Cometh*. "It was the turning point of my life," he recalled. "The awesome power of the play, the performances, everything and everyone was just so intense—something inside of me just clicked. By the end of the night, I had a goal in life." Hanks' new goal led him to a stage carpenter scholarship to California State University in Sacramento.

"By the end of the night...

... I had a goal in life."

Tom decided the experience was worth it. He, Samantha, and three others packed their cars and headed east to Cleveland. Tom never returned to Cal State. The first summer turned into three, and Tom threw himself into every part of the theater experience. He graduated from an unpaid intern in small parts to playing a variety of roles including Rosencrantz in *Hamlet* and Fabian in *Twelfth Night*. In 1978, a local drama critics group gave him their Best Actor designation for his role as Proteus in *The Two Gentlemen of Verona*. Ironically, it was one of the few times Tom played a bad guy.

"Being an actor was fun," he said. "You'd hang around, get into makeup and wardrobe, and go onstage under those amber gels—that was very romantic." The stage wasn't the only place for romance in Tom's life, however. He and Samantha were married in 1978. Shortly after the wedding, they headed to New York City to make it as actors.

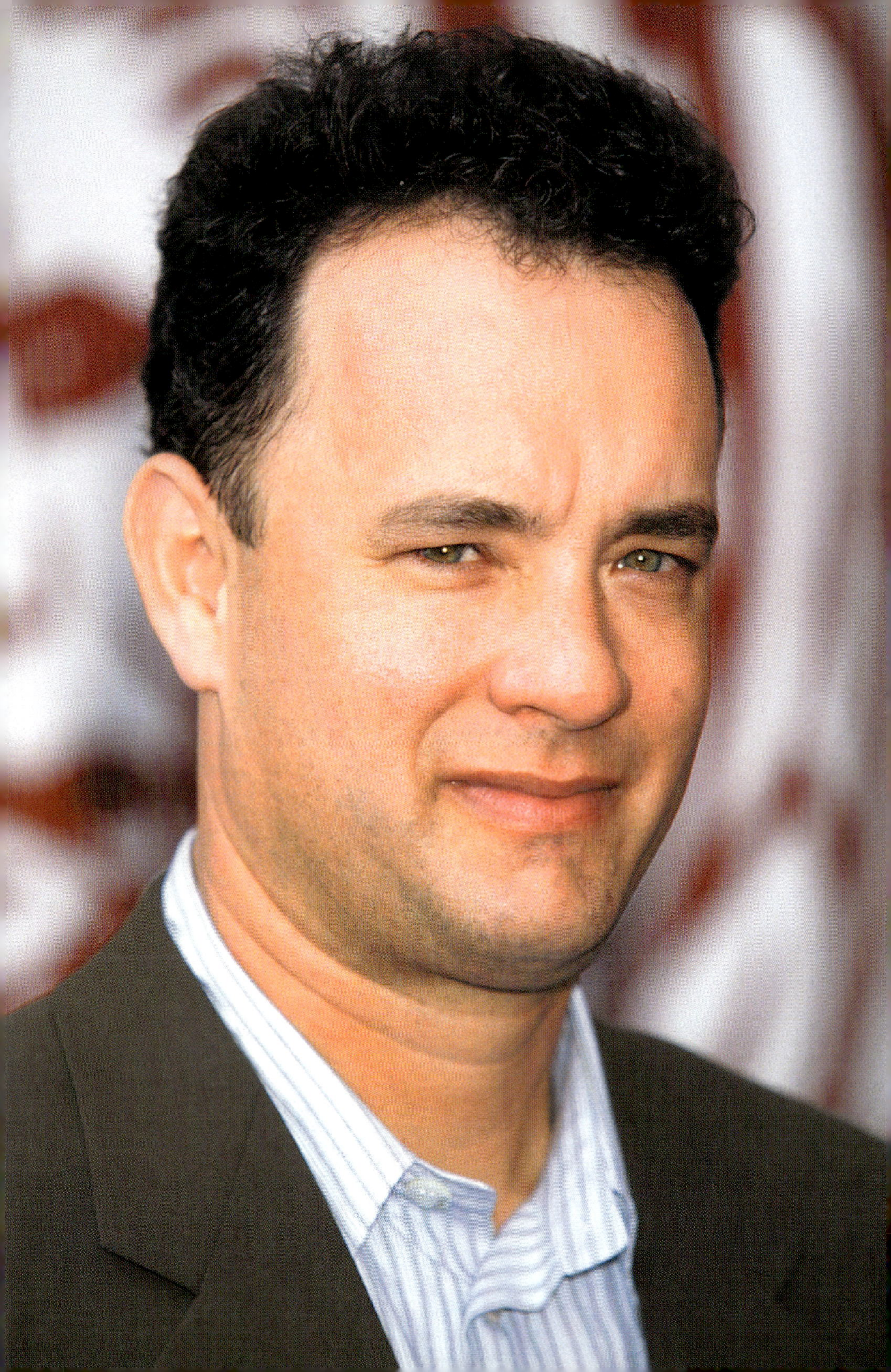

BOSOM BUDDIES

IN THE BIG APPLE, TOM JOINED THE Riverside Shakespeare Company as an unpaid actor. He collected unemployment while he worked for the company and looked for other paying acting jobs. Once he rehearsed four weekends for a gig that earned him only $25. By that time, he and Samantha had a son, Colin. Now Tom had two others to support. Fortunately, he found an agent to help him.

In 1979, Tom returned to the Great Lakes Shakespeare Festival for one more season. Upon completing that, he returned to New York for a part in his first movie. It was a small role in a low-budget slasher film called *He Knows You're Alone*. He followed that with the leading role in a made-for-TV movie called *Mazes and Monsters* based on the novel of the same name.

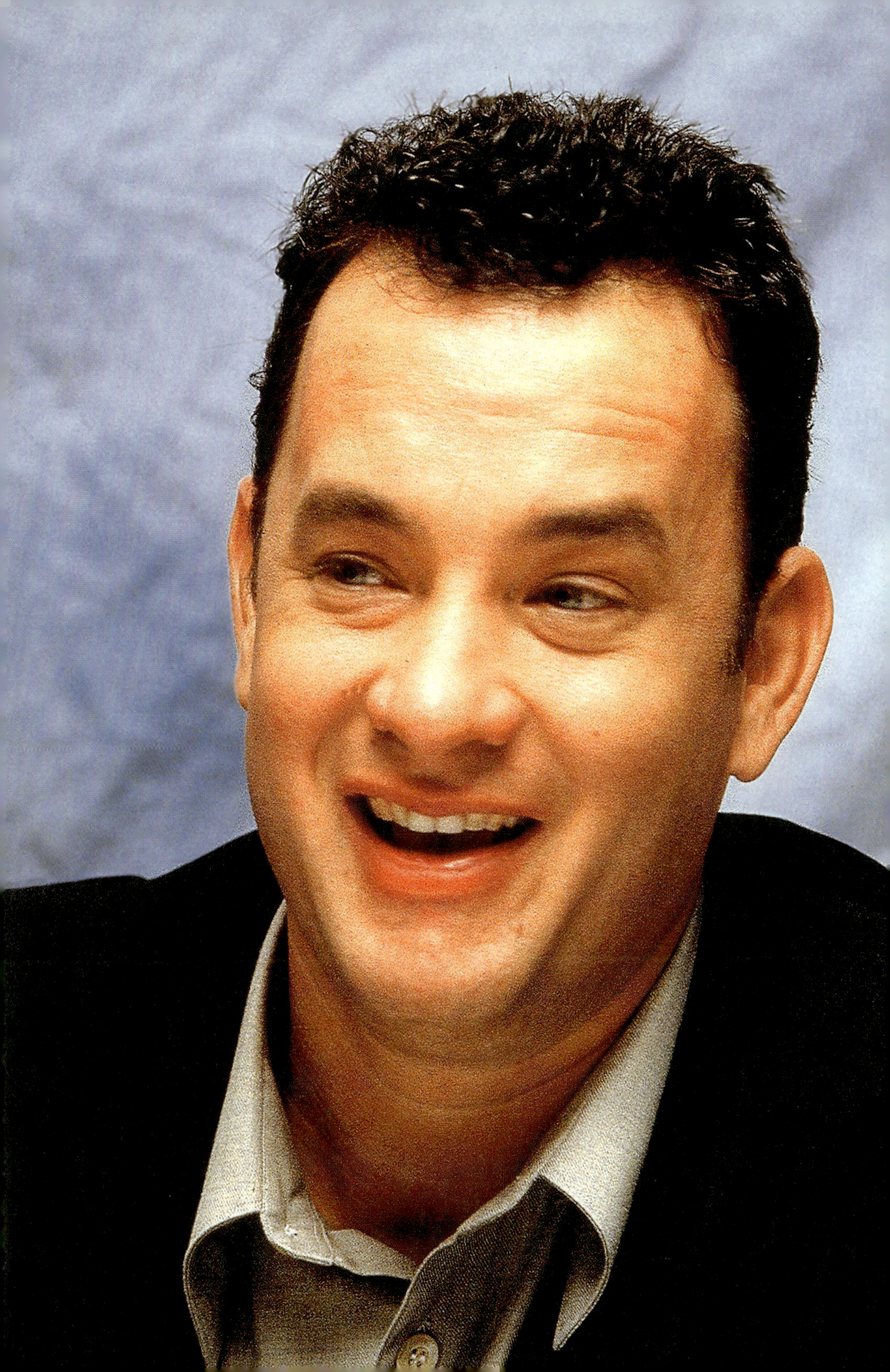

"I had no idea what I was getting into."

Neither movie made so much as a ripple among critics and audiences. Yet Tom's performance in *Mazes and Monsters* was enough to get him into auditions with ABC TV for various roles in their upcoming season. "I went on the initial 'go-see' with thousands of other people," Tom recalled. "The next thing I knew I was flying to Los Angeles and reading for the pilot of a show about a couple of guys who dress in drag in order to move into a women's hotel."

Tom got the part, and the pilot became a series called *Bosom Buddies*. It debuted on November 27, 1980. The quick switch from stage actor to TV performer took Hanks by surprise. "I thought that if I was going to make a living, it was going to be in regional theater," he said. "I had no idea what I was getting into; if somebody had told me, I would probably have choked." On the upside, he now was making $9,000 per episode. It was a big change from doing Shakespeare for free. It was also a good thing, as he and Samantha added daughter Elizabeth to their family in 1981.

Tom played the part of Kip Wilson, an advertising executive who dresses like a woman so he can live at a women's hotel. ABC produced 38 episodes that aired over a span of two years. Together with co-star Peter Scolari, Tom forced critics to admit that while the concept of the show was tired at times, the acting was exceptional. Tom and Peter enjoyed chemistry on-screen that had them ad-libbing to an already well-written script.

The discipline of a regular series also helped Tom hone his acting skills. When the series ended, however, he was back on his own. He took guest appearances on a number of TV series, including *Family Ties*, *Taxi,* and *Happy Days*. On the *Happy Days* set, he met a young actor and director named Ron Howard. Howard remembered Tom when it came to casting a movie he was working on.

Bosom Buddies

24 Star Tracks

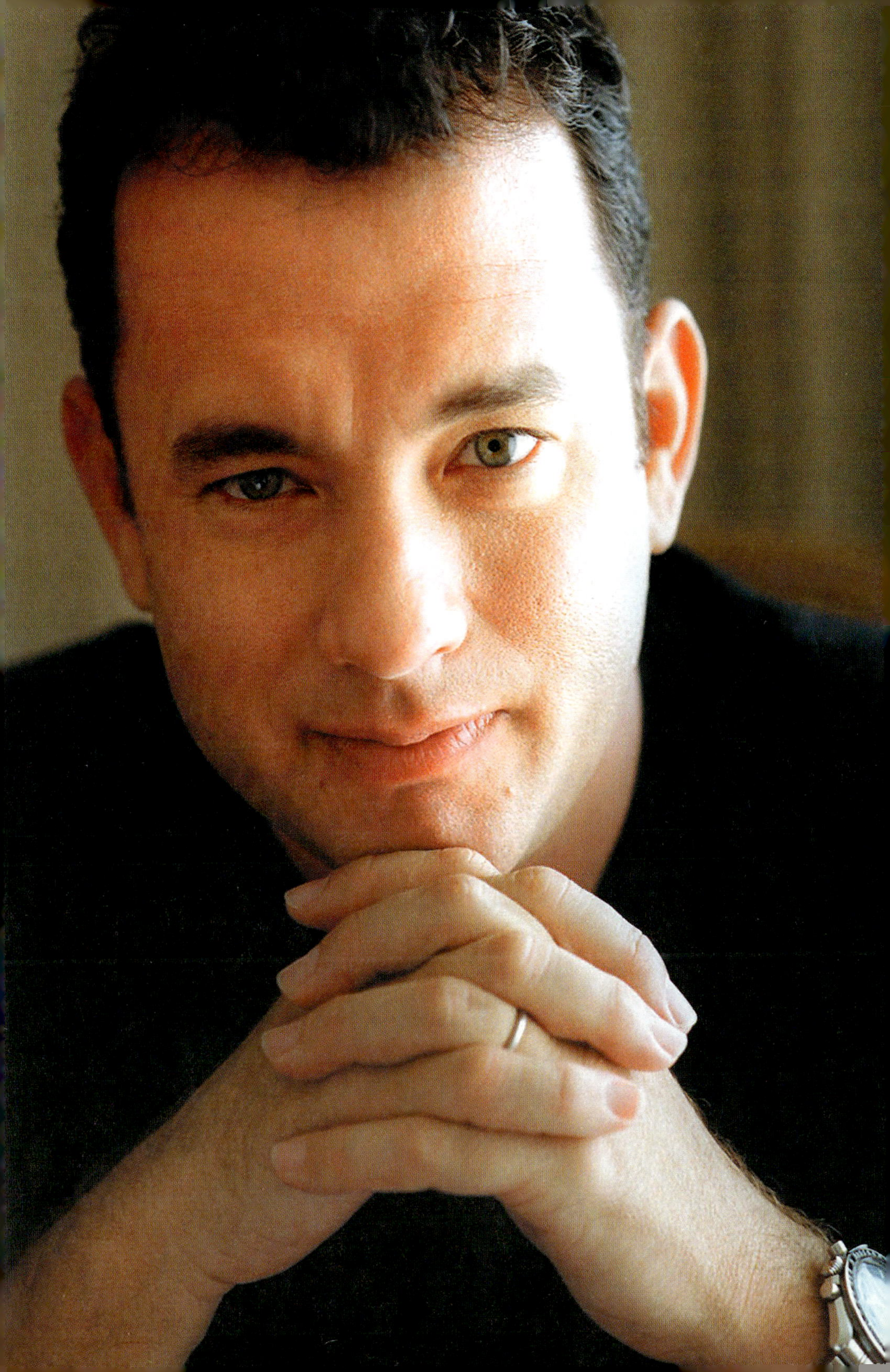

MAKING A SPLASH

THE MOVIE THAT RON HOWARD WAS developing was about a mermaid who falls in love with a normal man. "We tried to get Michael Keaton, we tried to get John Travolta, tried to get Bill Murray…" remembered Ron Howard about the casting process. "They were all unavailable or not interested. The word was real good on Tom Hanks around town. He read, and he was terrific. We just stopped looking."

In *Splash*, Tom played opposite Daryl Hannah and John Candy. Originally, Howard had Tom in mind for a supporting role, but he changed his mind and gave him the lead. Tom said the role was the hardest one yet for him. "I had to be Jimmy Stewart in *Splash*, goofy-looking but also relatively attractive, lovable, but mostly vulnerable…"

Tom Hanks and Helen Hunt, stars in the drama Cast Away, *pose together at the film's premiere in Los Angeles, December 7, 2000.*

DISCARDED

Splash

Crewmembers shot the film on location in New York City and the Bahamas, where the underwater scenes took place. "I found myself pounding on my chest, which was the hand signal for 'I need air,'" Tom said. "I grew up in awe of Jacques Cousteau and the *American Sportsman* shows. Scuba was something I would maybe do on a dare... But as a job I found the diving a real challenge."

Splash hit theaters in March 1984. The film was a hit among critics and filmgoers alike, taking in $24 million in its first 17 days. Once again, Tom was taken by surprise. One film—the right film—had made him a star.

Before *Splash* was even finished, Tom agreed to star in another movie called *Bachelor Party*. He began filming the comedy after his family moved to California. In the film, Tom played a bus driver about to marry a rich and beautiful woman. The story is about what happens when his friends throw him a party the night before the wedding.

Tom took the role not knowing how successful *Splash* would be. *Bachelor Party* was nowhere near the quality of *Splash*, and box office receipts showed it. Amazingly, Tom's reputation survived. The entertainment magazine *Variety* said the main reason to see the movie was "for Hanks' performance. Recalling a younger Bill Murray, Hanks is all over the place, practically spilling off the screen with an overabundance of energy."

Tom Hanks' star on the Walk of Fame in Hollywood.

HITS AND MISSES

FOR THE NEXT FIVE YEARS, TOM KEPT cranking out comedies. After wrapping *Bachelor Party* in the summer of 1984, he headed to Washington, D.C., to do a remake of a popular French film. The remake was called *The Man with One Red Shoe*. Tom played the lead—a violinist who gets caught between two rival groups within the Central Intelligence Agency (CIA). For the part, Tom spent three months learning to play the violin. He also talked to many musicians to find out what it was like to be one.

As soon as that film was finished, Tom headed to southern Mexico for a new film. In *Volunteers*, he played a spoiled upper-class man who joins the Peace Corps to escape some gambling debts. The job takes him to Thailand where he's to help a crew of volunteers build a bridge.

Tom Hanks displays his 1998 People's Choice Award for All Time Favorite Motion Picture Actor.

"I've learned to accept **personal failure** without being completely demoralized by it…"

At first, Tom's character, Lawrence Bourne III, wants nothing to do with the project. Then he meets another volunteer, played by Rita Wilson. He wants to win Rita's heart, so he decides to show her he's not such a bad guy after all. By the end of the film, he's even willing to risk his life to help the local villagers.

The Man with One Red Shoe opened in theaters in July 1985. *Volunteers* opened just one week later. The first film was a box-office disaster. *Volunteers* didn't make much money, either, though it received mixed reviews. Most critics agreed Hanks was the highlight of *Volunteers*. Tom didn't let the negatives get in his way.

"I've learned to accept personal failure without being completely demoralized by it for long periods of time," Tom said. "You can't let that bad dog follow you around for the rest of your life." And he didn't. He quickly signed on for a new Steven Spielberg film called *The Money Pit*.

The Money Pit is about a couple who buys a house together and begin fixing it up. In the film, Tom played opposite *Cheers* star Shelley Long. The movie combines the romance between Tom and Shelley and the slapstick comedy of a broken-down house. As it turned out, Tom and Shelley's relationship took a back seat to the crumbling house.

Critics were quick to pick that up when the movie opened Christmas 1985. While Tom tried to inject warmth into the film, the special affects and sight gags of the house overshadowed it.

Despite the lukewarm reviews, Columbia Pictures offered him a deal to star in some of its new films. The first was a dramatic comedy called *Nothing in Common* in which Tom starred with veteran performer Jackie Gleason. The role required him to go from generating laughs to generating tears. He did both.

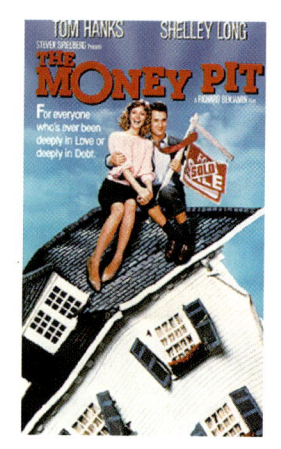

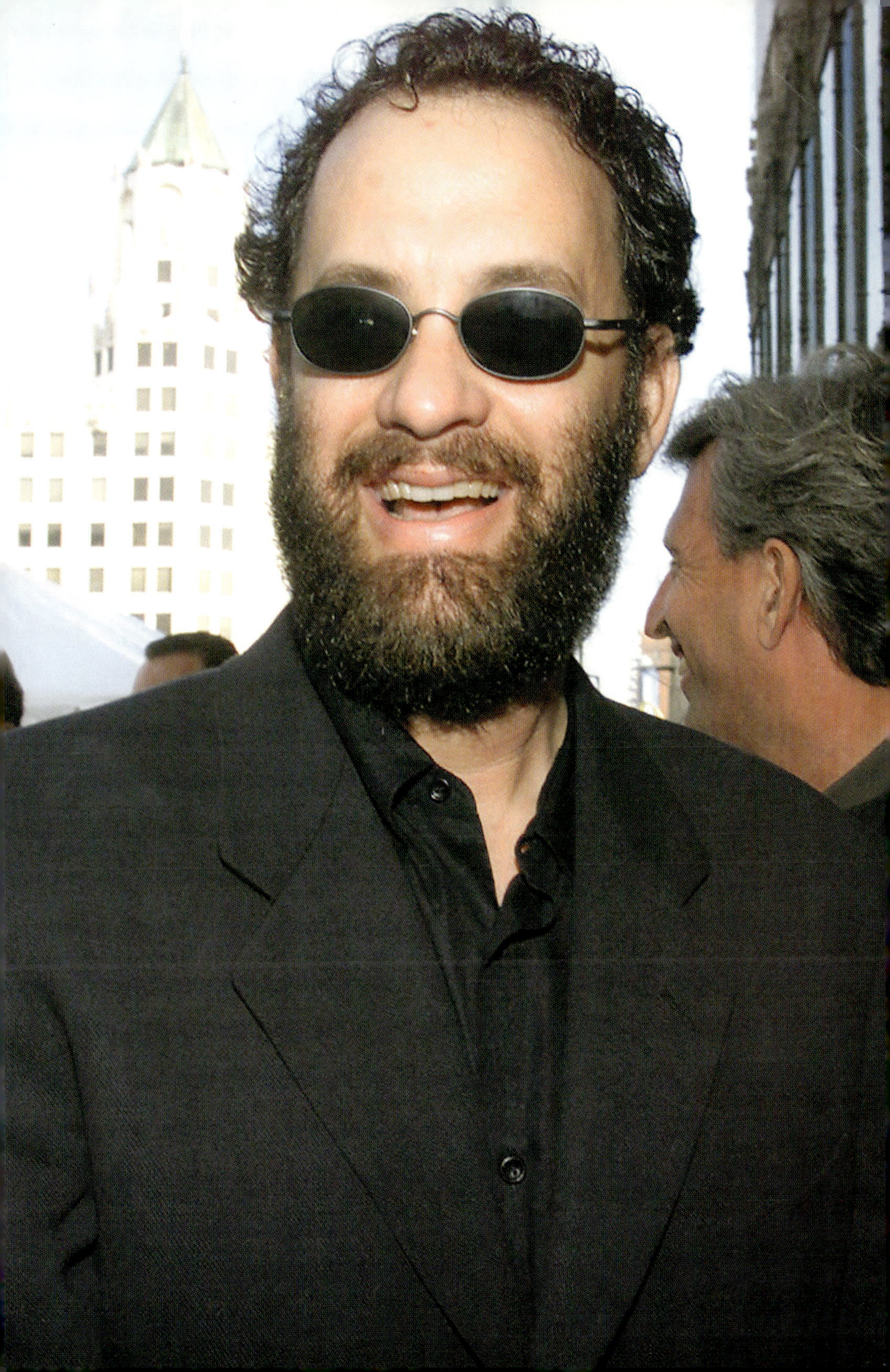

Tom Hanks and his wife, actress Rita Wilson, arrive as guests for the Women of Courage Awards benefit dinner for the Cedars-Sinai Research for Women's Cancers support group March 28, 2000, in Beverly Hills, CA. Hanks' beard was for his upcoming film Cast Away.

A FINE ROMANCE

WHILE TOM'S CAREER WAS CHARGING full-speed ahead, his marriage was floundering. Wife Samantha, taking care of two children while Tom traveled around the country filming movies, felt her career had stalled. Tom tried to help by co-producing a play with her. Samantha also played a role in the play. It wasn't enough. The two separated while Tom was filming *Nothing in Common*.

Tom always had kept his personal life to himself. This turn of events was no exception. "My work didn't ruin my marriage," he said in an interview with the *Los Angeles Times*. "You can't put the blame on the film business. It's just as hard working at a bank and staying happily married as it is doing movies."

Tom quickly headed to Israel to film a new movie. *Every Time We Say Goodbye* was the story of an American pilot during World War II who falls in love with a young Jewish girl. Because of her religion, the girl cannot be with Tom's character. It was Tom's first serious, dramatic role.

Neither critics nor audiences cared for Tom in that role. However, *Nothing in Common* had hit theaters and been a moderate success. Tom's other success was in his personal life. His relationship with *Volunteers* co-star Rita Wilson was blossoming. The two showed up together at the Academy Awards ceremony in March 1987. On New Year's Eve 1987, he proposed. "We were all at this table together," he told *Vanity Fair* magazine. "I had just asked Rita to marry me and she said, 'You bet!'"

Tom and Rita were married in April 1988. The year before, Tom had released the successful movie *Dragnet,* in which he starred with Dan Akroyd. In summer 1988, he again would be in two movies for the summer season. One would put him back on top in Hollywood.

Tom Hanks and his wife, Rita Wilson, arrive at the Waldorf-Astoria Hotel in New York, April 29, 1999. The American Museum of the Moving Image saluted Hanks for his contributions to the movie industry.

Tom Hanks 39

COMEBACK

TOM WAS NOT DIRECTOR PENNY Marshall's first choice to play the young boy who finds himself in a grown-up body in *Big*. Yet after the movie opened in spring 1988, few people could imagine anyone but Tom in the role of Josh Baskin. Audiences and critics alike marveled at how Tom could act like a child as well as he did. Tom's scene playing "Chopsticks" on a giant floor piano is now a classic in cinema.

"I remember 12 being all elbows and knees," Tom told the *New York Times* about preparing for his role. "The girls had already grown up. I started the role with the point of view of a newborn giraffe."

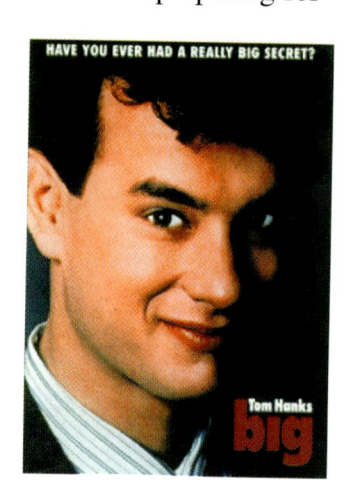

Tom Hanks poses with his Best Actor award for Cast Away, at the 58th Annual Golden Globe Awards in Beverly Hills, CA, January 21, 2001.

Big was a smash hit, earning $110 million at the box office. It overshadowed his movie *Punchline* that, though filmed earlier, hit theaters after *Big*.

Big landed Tom on the cover of *Newsweek* and earned him a second stint as the guest host on *Saturday Night Live*. The role also earned him his first Golden Globe for best performance in a comedy and a nomination for the Best Actor Oscar. The Oscar went to Dustin Hoffman for *Rain Man*, yet it was only a matter of time before it would be Tom's turn.

Big earned Tom Hanks his first Golden Globe award, plus an Academy Award nomination for Best Actor.

Tom Hanks with writer Stephen King at the premiere of The Green Mile *in New York City, December 8, 1999.*

44 Star Tracks

Tom's career thus far seemed to be under the care of a guardian angel. Despite some obvious flops, movie offers kept coming in. After *Big*, Tom was ensnared in several more lukewarm films—*Turner & Hooch,* where he co-starred with a dog, *The 'burbs*, a dark comedy about suburban life, and *Joe Versus the Volcano*.

Joe was about a terminally ill man who agrees to a strange deal. He can live like a king for a while as long as he jumps into a volcano at the end of the stint. The movie was a flop, yet it paired him with actress Meg Ryan. Audiences saw the beginning of a wonderful chemistry between the two that would get more play in the future.

Joe Versus the Volcano

Tom Hanks **45**

Perhaps the worst role thus far came in 1990 in Brian DePalma's *Bonfire of the Vanities*. Critics agreed Tom was horribly miscast as a successful Wall Street executive whose life turns into a nightmare after a hit-and-run accident involving a young African-American man. The film cost $60 million to make, and even Tom's talents couldn't save it.

After *Bonfire*, Tom took two years off from the business. "I had worked myself into a hole," he said. "I also think there was a chance the American public was gonna get sick of looking at me. I'd been out there with a new movie every spring and again every summer for a lot of years and you can easily overstay your welcome." Tom and Rita took advantage of the break to start their own family with the birth of son Chester. Later they would add another son, Truman.

When the break was up, Tom worked again with director Penny Marshall on *A League of Their Own*. The movie is the story of the professional women's baseball league formed during World War II. Tom plays Jimmy Duggan, a washed-up baseball player brought in to manage one of the teams. He gained 25 pounds for the role and won America's heart once again with his gruff-but-good-hearted character.

President Bill Clinton, Winifred Lancy, a 101-year-old mother whose son was killed in WWII, and Tom Hanks at the WWII Memorial during the groundbreaking ceremony on the National Mall in Washington, D.C., October 11, 2000.

AND THE OSCAR GOES TO...

NOW BACK ON TRACK, TOM SIGNED UP for another winning role in Nora Ephron's *Sleepless in Seattle* with his *Joe Versus the Volcano* co-star Meg Ryan. The two worked magic on the screen as a widower and his long-distance soulmate. The film became a surprise hit in summer 1993.

Riding high on the success of *Sleepless*, Tom took on his toughest role yet. He began preparing to play the role of high-powered lawyer Andrew Beckett, who contracts AIDS in *Philadelphia*. Beckett is fired by his law firm and feels he was fired because of his illness. He seeks the help of an attorney, played by Denzel Washington, to sue for discrimination.

Tom Hanks after winning the Best Actor Oscar for Philadelphia.

Best Actor winner Tom Hanks gives an emotional speech at the 66th Annual Academy Awards in Los Angeles, on March 21, 1994.

The role of Andrew was controversial because the character is gay. Yet Tom viewed the story as appealing to a wide audience. "This is the story of a man who has been done wrong and wants justice," he said. "We're talking about a guy who was robbed and he wants to get back what was taken from him. I think there's nobody who can't relate to that."

Tom lost 35 pounds and had his hair thinned to play Andrew. He talked to people who had AIDS and asked them what it was like. When the film opened in 1993, Tom gave the performance of a lifetime. He was rewarded with another Golden Globe Award and two months later, his first Best Actor Oscar.

In his acceptance speech, Tom recognized his high school drama teacher, who was gay, as a major influence in his acting career. He went on to pay a tribute to the thousands of people who had died from AIDS. "I know that my work in this case is magnified by the fact that the streets of heaven are too crowded with angels," he said. His moving speech brought the audience to their feet and brought many people to tears.

IN THE DIRECTOR'S CHAIR

IT WAS HARD TO IMAGINE THERE WAS any role that would bring more recognition to Tom than *Philadelphia*. Yet it happened when Tom teamed with director Robert Zemekis. Zemekis had directed all three *Back to the Future* movies, along with *Who Framed Roger Rabbit*?

This time the project was *Forrest Gump*. The movie was based on a novel about a mildly retarded man who goes on to become a football star, a Vietnam war hero, a successful shrimp boat captain, and more. The film was a huge success, earning more than $300 million in 1994. It also earned Tom his second Best Actor Oscar. That made him only the second man ever to achieve such an accomplishment. Spencer Tracey was the first when he won back-to-back Oscars in 1937 and 1938.

Tom Hanks as Forrest Gump.

That Thing You Do

From *Forrest Gump*, Tom returned to working behind the scenes. He wrote, directed, and acted in *That Thing You Do*, the story of a small-town band that hits it big. "I thought I knew what this was like from being an actor," Tom said about the directing business. "It's totally different to be the guy who wrote it and all this stuff. It's not as much fun."

Apollo 13

Director Tom Hanks on the set of the HBO mini series From The Earth To The Moon. *The mini series was nominated for an Emmy in 1998.*

He got back into the fun with his next film, *Apollo 13*. It was a dream role for Tom, who had wanted to be an astronaut as a little boy. He loved filming the movie, even though he had to practice zero gravity with rides in a plane dubbed the "Vomit Comet" because it made people sick.

He also had a chance to try something new as the voice for Woody in the animated film *Toy Story*. He reprised the role as the voice of Woody again in the 1999 sequel *Toy Story 2*.

MAXIMUM STAR POWER

TWENTY YEARS AFTER HIS FIRST MOVIE role, Tom is among the most sought-after actors of Hollywood's directing set. He teamed up with director Steven Spielberg again for 1998's powerhouse *Saving Private Ryan*. The internationally acclaimed film won five Academy Awards. Its graphic portrayal of the Allied invasion of Europe in World War II was a powerful reminder of the horrors of war.

You've Got Mail

Saving Private Ryan

Director Nora Ephron pegged Tom again for the male lead in her successful film, *You've Got Mail*. Tom teamed up again with Meg Ryan, generating comparisons of them as the new Katherine Hepburn/Spencer Tracey duo. Tom followed that success with a critically acclaimed role in *The Green Mile*.

Not only is Tom popular with directors, but he's also popular with fans. When asked for the reason behind his appeal, he replied in his usual lighthearted manner. "I would hope it's because I'm fascinating, interesting, charming, witty, funny and yet… can be taken seriously," he said. "Actually, I have no idea. I couldn't figure it out in a million years. Nor would I want to. I do what I do."

In 2000, Tom played the lead in *Cast Away*. He lost 70 pounds for the film to look like he was starving. *Cast Away* was another huge hit for Tom, earning him a Golden Globe Award and an Oscar Nomination.

Tom Hanks puts his hands in the cement in front of Mann's Chinese Theater in Hollywood, as his wife Rita Wilson watches on July 23, 1998.

For Christmas 2001, Tom is scheduled to play the conductor in the movie version of the popular children's book *The Polar Express*. Knowing Tom Hanks, it will be another express ride to the top of the box office charts.

Disney · PIXAR
TOY STORY 2
RACING TEAM
-Woody
Hugs & Kisses
Love
BO
XOXOXO
Jessie
BUZZ
94
TAURUS
ROUSH Racing
MOOG
SELECT
CLEVITE
SIMPSON
Edelbrock
plasti-kote
76
WIX

Tom Hanks and co-star Tim Allen on a promo tour for Toy Story 2.

WHERE ON THE WEB?

You can find out more about Tom Hanks by visiting the following web sites. Or, check the sites for his latest films:

Tom Hanks on Mr. Showbiz
http//mrshowbiz.go.com/people/tomhanks/index.html

Tom Hanks, a Biography
http://www.moviething.com/bios/tomhanks/

GO Entertainment Tom Hanks Profile
http://www.entertainment.go.com/people/tomhanks/index.html

Digital Hit Entertainment's Celebrity Row
http://www.digitalhit.com/tomhanks.shtml

Fans also can write to Tom Hanks at:
Tom Hanks c/o PMK
955 S. Carillo Drive, Suite 200
Los Angeles, California 90048

GLOSSARY

Academy Awards: The top awards given out each year for artistic and technical achievement in motion pictures.

Oscar: The gold statuette given to those receiving an Academy Award.

Pilot: The first episode of a television show. If enough viewers like a pilot, additional episodes are produced.

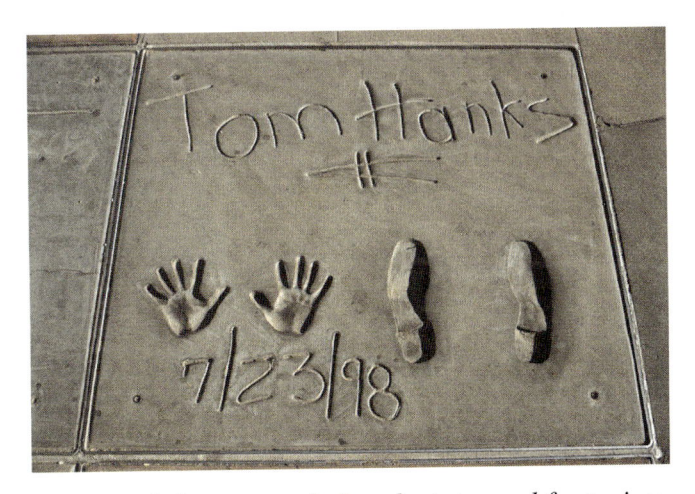

Tom Hanks' autograph, handprints, and footprints pressed into the cement in the sidewalk outside of Mann's Chinese Theater in Hollywood.

INDEX

A
A League of Their Own 7, 46
ABC TV 23, 24
Academy Awards 38, 56
Akroyd, Dan 38
American Sportsman 28
Apollo 13 55

B
Bachelor Party 28, 29, 30
Back to the Future 52
Big 20, 40, 42, 45
Bonfire of the Vanities 46
Bosom Buddies 23
'burbs, The 45

C
California State University 14, 17, 18
Cast Away 58
Central Intelligence Agency 30
Chabot Junior College 10, 12
Chekhov, Anton 17
Cheers 34
Cherry Orchard, The 17
Cleveland, OH 17, 18
Columbia Pictures 34
Concord, CA 8
Cousteau, Jacques 28

D
Dowling, Vincent 17
Dragnet 38

E
Ephron, Nora 48, 58

Every Time We Say Goodbye 38

F
Family Ties 24
Forrest Gump 52, 54

G
Gleason, Jackie 34
Golden Globe 42, 51, 58
Grant, Cary 4
Great Lakes Shakespeare Festival 17, 20
Green Mile, The 58

H
Hamlet 18
Hanks, Amos 8
Hanks, Chester 46
Hanks, Colin 20
Hanks, Elizabeth 23
Hanks, Janet 8
Hanks, Truman 46
Hannah, Daryl 26
Happy Days 24
Hayward, CA 10
He Knows You're Alone 20
Hepburn, Katherine 58
Hoffman, Dustin 42
Howard, Ron 7, 24, 26

I
Iceman Cometh, The 14
Israel 38

J
Joe Versus the Volcano 45, 48

K
Keaton, Michael 26

L
Lemmon, Jack 7

Lewes, Samantha 17, 18, 20, 23, 37
Long, Shelley 34
Los Angeles, CA 23, 62
Los Angeles Times 37

M
Man with One Red Shoe, The 30, 33
Marshall, Penny 7, 40, 46
Mazes and Monsters 23
Money Pit, The 33, 34
Murray, Bill 26, 29

N
New York City, NY 18, 20, 28
New York Times 40
Newsweek 42
Nothing in Common 34, 37, 38

O
Oakland, CA 10
Oscar 42, 51, 52, 58

P
Peace Corps 30
Philadelphia 48, 52
Polar Express, The 59
Punchline 42

R
Rain Man 42
Riverside Shakespeare Company 20
Ryan, Meg 45, 48, 58

S
Sacramento, CA 14
Saturday Night Live 42

Saving Private Ryan 56
Scolari, Peter 24
Sleepless in Seattle 48
South Pacific 10
Spielberg, Steven 33, 56
Splash 7, 26, 28, 29
Stewart, Jimmy 4, 7, 26

T
Taxi 24
Thailand 30
That Thing You Do 54
Toy Story 55
Toy Story 2 55
Tracey, Spencer 52, 58
Travolta, John 26
Turner & Hooch 45
Twelfth Night 18
Two Gentlemen of Verona, The 18

V
Vanity Fair 38
Variety 29
Volunteers 30, 33, 38

W
Washington, D.C. 30
Washington, Denzel 48
Who Framed Roger Rabbit? 52
Wilson, Rita 33, 38

Y
You've Got Mail 58

Z
Zemekis, Robert 52